Rory Margraf

Stille Nacht
Silent Night

The Story of the Christmas Truce

Illustrated by Andreea Mironiuc

Illustrated by Andreea Mironiuc
www.andreeamironiuc.com

ISBN: 979-8-218-11625-5

For Dad, who taught me the importance of history and lessons from humanity.

Among the trees of France sat a field
where nothing lived.

No birds, no deer, no mice nor serpent.

No man nor woman lived on this land.

It was No Man's Land.

But there was life in these woods.

Two great armies sat
in cold trenches dug into
the frozen earth.

Brothers in humanity, enemies by order, they waited for the terrible whistle, commanding them to charge into the land that no man could claim.

But, on this day, no whistle was blown,
no command was given.

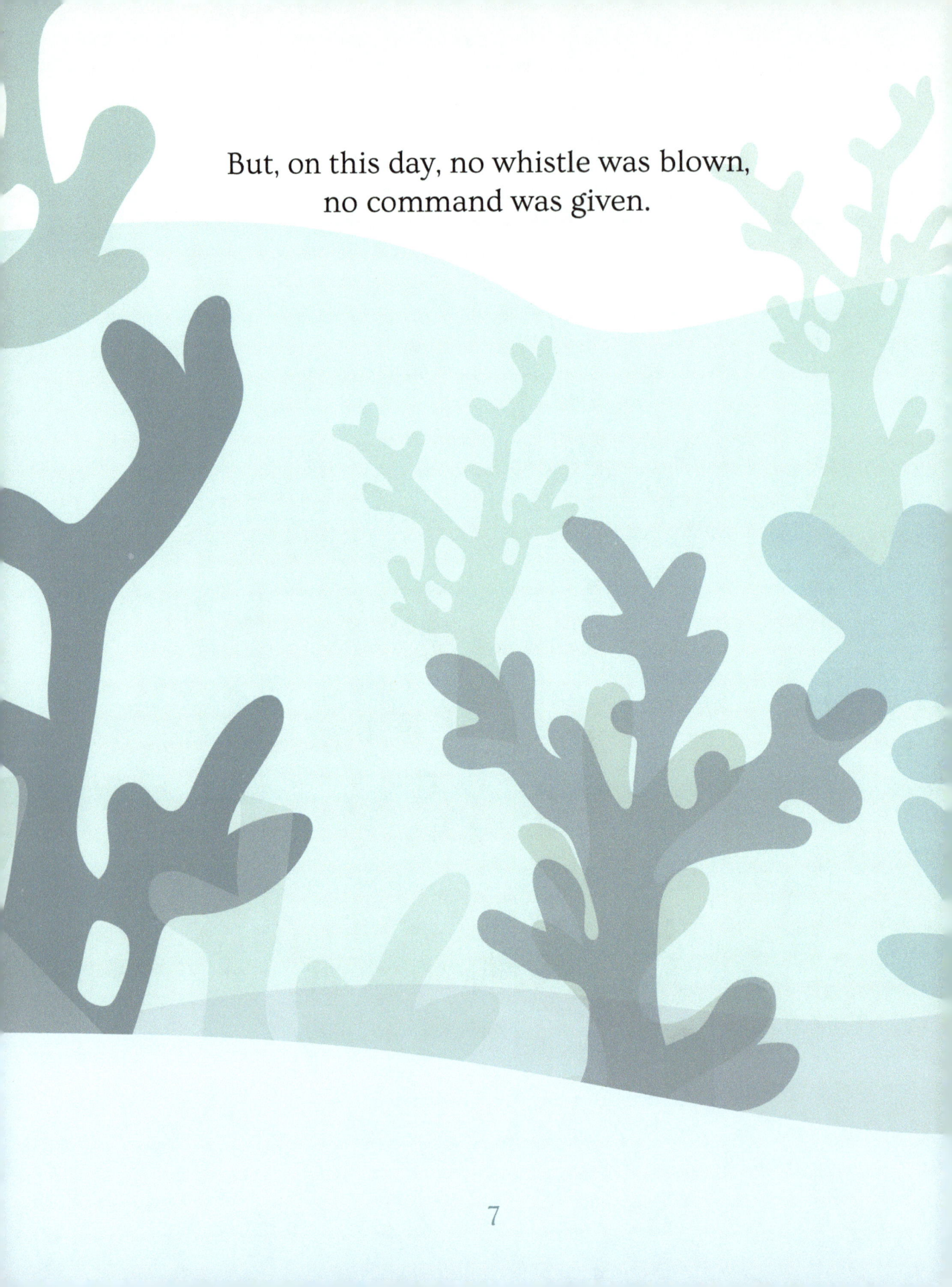

On this day, the land lay silent.

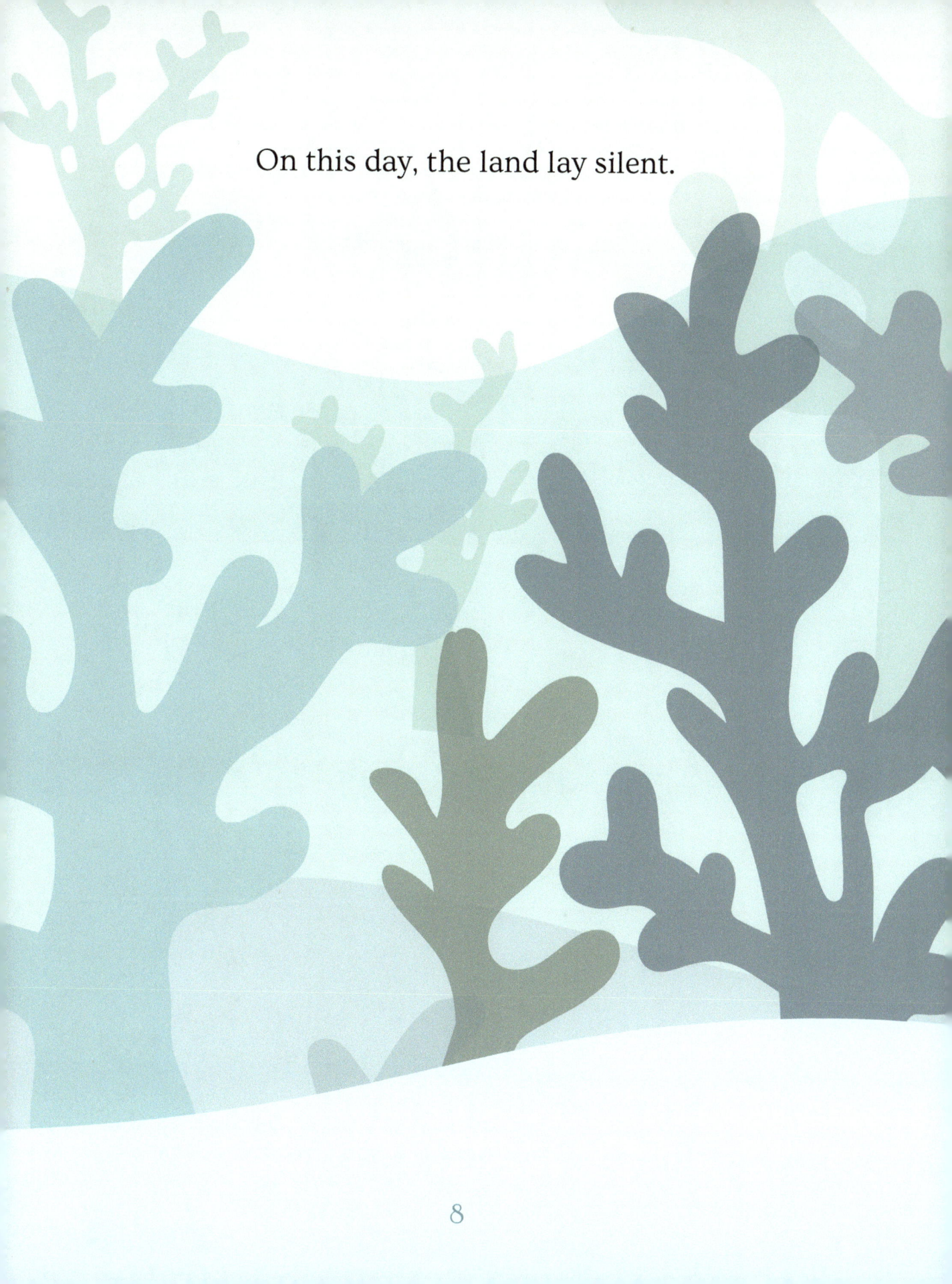

A new blanket of snow rested lightly over the field,
hiding the earth, burned and torn by
man's terrible weapons.

From the trenches, suddenly, came a sound this land had never heard before.

A quiet laugh had escaped from beneath the earth!

Ha

Ha

Ha

Ha

Ha

Ha

Ha

Ha

Ha

Ha

Ha

Ha   Ha

The sound made its way through the trenches and the laughter soon grew and spread across the land.

Suddenly, a smiling soldier lifted his head above the trench and peered across the land.

Ha

Ha

Ha

Ha

Ha

Ha

Ha
Ha
Ha
Ha Ha
Ha
Ha
Ha

He saw no enemy and, with a trembling hand, slowly climbed out of the trench and placed his boot in the snow.

His comrades watched silently as he walked across the land, his weapon left behind.

Each step he took was firm, for a weaker step
would send him back to safety.

As he reached the center, he slowed and looked
across the land, with hands held out in waiting.

In the distance, he looked, seeking a sign of life.
Suddenly, a helmet emerged from the trenches with
a man rising beneath.

The soldier walked through the snow and soon the two enemies stood face to face, alone in the tired field.

"Merry Christmas," said one, his voice strained by the winter air and shaking with fear.

A moment passed, and a smile soon grew across the other soldier's face. "Merry Christmas," he said in his own language.

Ha
Ha
Ha
Ha
Ha
Ha
Ha
Ha

The two great armies watched
these men carefully and
soon heard their laughter from
across the land.

The land that could hold no living thing was soon filled with life as hundreds of men emerged, meeting their enemy, greeting them as old friends.

Well wishes were made as
different languages filled the air.

Hands were shaken, hugs were given,
laughter was shared.

A soldier began to point frantically at another, gesturing to the buttons on his uniform.

Moving his hands quickly, he hoped that his words would be understood.

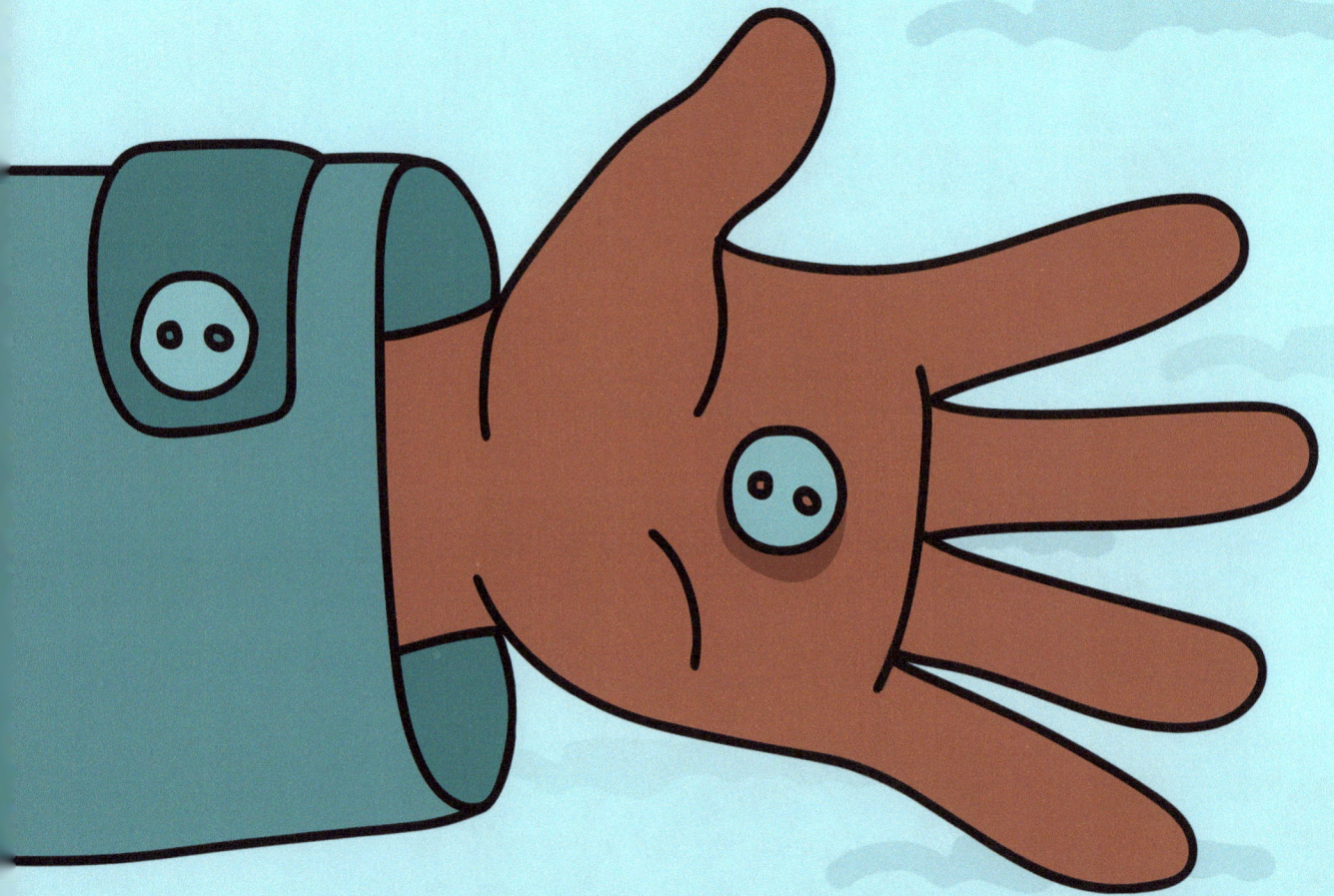

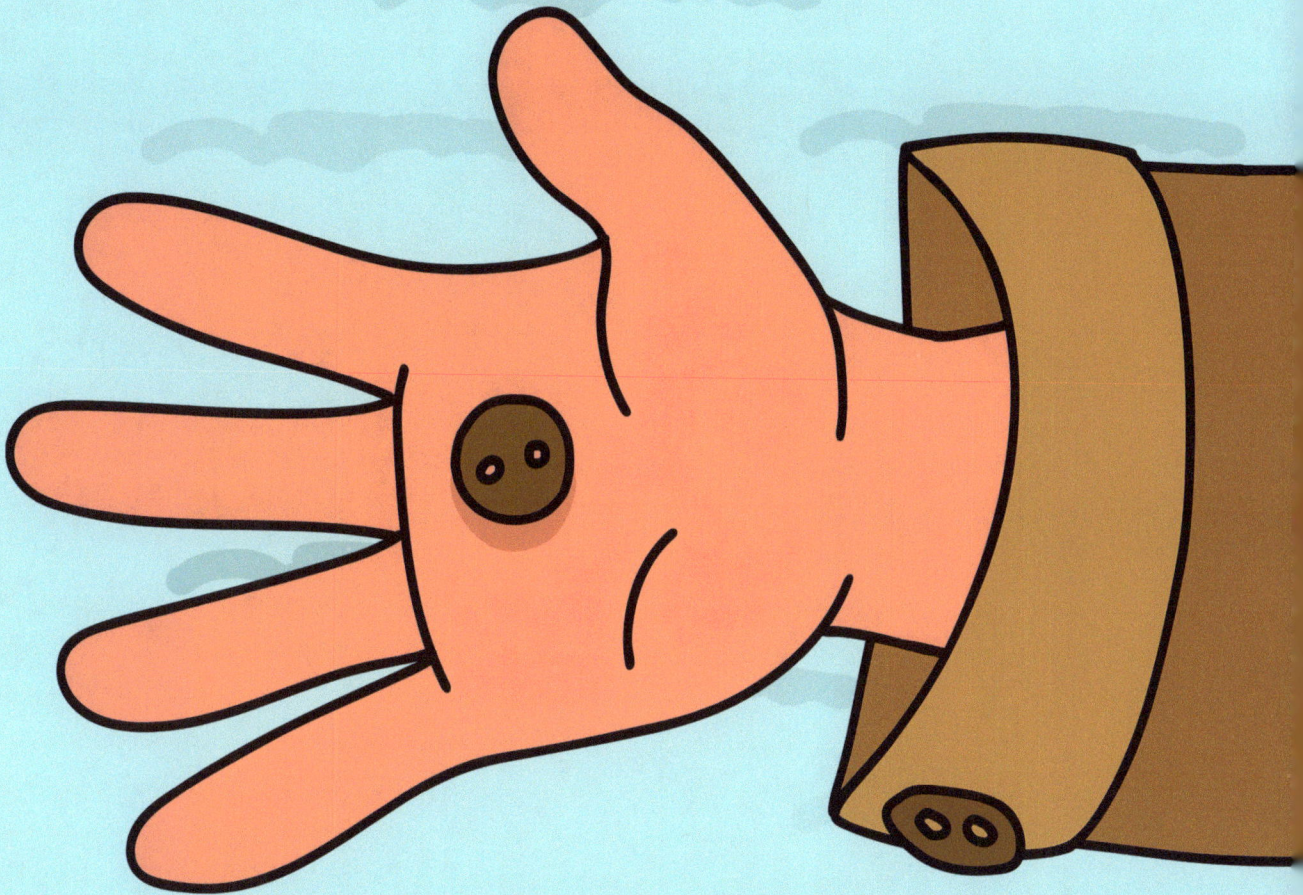

His enemy watched in earnest. Suddenly, he knew!

He plucked a button off of his uniform and handed it
to the soldier, who took his own button off and
quickly exchanged the gift.

And as the land filled with soldiers, what began?

A soccer game!

Helmets and uniforms, flags and weapons were tossed aside as an old beef tin became the ball!

No score was kept, and no winner was declared, but hands were shaken, and hugs were exchanged.

As the land filled with song and joy, the sun began to set, and the air grew colder.

The shadows grew and a familiar silence began to cover the land.

The soldiers looked back towards their trenches
and weapons and then to their enemy,
now friends and brothers.

With weary smiles, goodbyes were said,
hands were shaken, hugs were given, and final gifts
were exchanged.

The snow fell lightly over the land as these two
great armies returned to their trenches.

Their bones chilled by the winter air; their spirits
warmed by the joy they had received.

For one day, this cold, lifeless land was filled with warmth and love. Commanded to be enemies, two great armies found humanity on the battlefield.

The war has long since ended, and the armies have retreated. But this land will forever hold a moment of peace in its soil and life will grow once more from the earth.

www.ingramcontent.com/pod-product-compliance
Lightning Source LLC
Chambersburg PA
CBHW041722040426
42449CB00025B/57